GREAT CAREERS IN EDUCATION

by Brienna Rossiter

FOCUS
READERS®

NAVIGATOR

WWW.FOCUSREADERS.COM

Focus Readers is distributed by North Star Editions:
sales@northstareditions.com | 888-417-0195

Produced for Focus Readers by Red Line Editorial.

Photographs ©: iStockphoto, cover, 1; Shutterstock Images, 4–5, 7, 8–9, 11, 13, 14–15, 17, 19, 20–21, 23, 25, 26–27; Red Line Editorial, 29

Library of Congress Cataloging-in-Publication Data
Names: Rossiter, Brienna, author.
Title: Great careers in education / by Brienna Rossiter.
Description: Lake Elmo, MN : Focus Readers, [2022] | Series: Great Careers | Includes index. | Audience: Grades 4-6
Identifiers: LCCN 2021009764 (print) | LCCN 2021009765 (ebook) | ISBN 9781644938423 (Hardcover) | ISBN 9781644938881 (Paperback) | ISBN 9781644939345 (eBook) | ISBN 9781644939765 (PDF)
Subjects: LCSH: Education--Vocational guidance--United States--Juvenile literature. | Teaching--Vocational guidance--United States--Juvenile literature.
Classification: LCC LB1775.2 .R73 2022 (print) | LCC LB1775.2 (ebook) | DDC 371.102/3--dc23
LC record available at https://lccn.loc.gov/2021009764
LC ebook record available at https://lccn.loc.gov/2021009765

Printed in the United States of America
Mankato, MN
082021

ABOUT THE AUTHOR

Brienna Rossiter is a writer and editor who lives in Minnesota. She enjoys learning about many subjects but especially likes facts about animals and science.

TABLE OF CONTENTS

CHAPTER 1

BEYOND THE CLASSROOM

When people think of careers in education, they often think of teachers at schools. But there are many other jobs related to education. People teach children in a variety of settings. Some people work with very young children at day cares. Tutors work with small groups of students. They help them

High school teachers often focus on a specific subject, such as science.

develop specific skills. For example, tutors might help with math or English.

Other people teach adults. Literacy teachers help people learn to read. GED teachers work with adults who did not finish high school. Career counselors help people find jobs. They give advice so that

ELL INSTRUCTORS

ELL stands for English Language Learner. ELL instructors teach English to people who do not speak it as their first language. Instructors can work with students of all ages. Sometimes they teach young children. Other times, they work with adults. Many ELL instructors teach in classrooms. Others work with individual students. They may even teach students online.

Some teachers help adults gain skills that will improve their careers.

people can build skills. Other workers help companies train their employees.

In addition, many workers help schools manage and track information. They plan schedules, **budgets**, and other details. Or they assist people with finding and applying to schools. All these jobs help people learn and grow.

CHAPTER 2

WORKING WITH STUDENTS

Many people interact with students during the school day. Some people make sure students have the skills and resources they need. One example is a school counselor. School counselors talk with students and help them solve problems. They also help students get ready to graduate. They assist students in

A counselor may help students figure out how to manage their time and study more effectively.

choosing classes and looking for colleges or jobs.

Special education is another example. These teachers focus on students with disabilities. Special ed students may have a variety of needs. The needs can be physical, mental, or behavioral. Special ed teachers help each student get an education that meets these needs. Sometimes they teach in a separate classroom. Other times, they help students in another teacher's class. They try to find what is best for each student.

Part of this work is creating an individualized education program (IEP). An IEP lists goals for the student. These

Special education teachers make sure all students have what they need to reach their goals.

goals can focus on learning or behavior. IEPs also describe the type of support students need to reach their goals. For example, students may need more time to take tests. Or they may need to work with a specialist. A speech-language pathologist (SLP) is one example. SLPs help treat problems with talking and communication. They meet with students. They make specific plans for each one.

In some cases, students work with aides. Aides help students with tasks during the day. For example, aides may help students stay focused or follow instructions. They may also help with

SOCIAL WORKERS

Many schools have social workers. These jobs focus on students who are having trouble at school. Problems may include bullying, poor grades, or missing class. Social workers try to find out what is causing each issue. They work with the students' families to make plans to help. In some cases, they **refer** students to therapists or other experts.

Part of a speech-language pathologist's job involves helping students improve their pronunciation.

hygiene. Some aides stay with students all day. Others help only at certain times. Whatever the role, these jobs ensure that students get the help they need to succeed.

CHAPTER 3

ADMINISTRATION

Administration jobs focus on the many details that help a school run. A principal or dean leads the school's staff and teachers. This person sets goals for the teachers and the school. Deans and principals create budgets and schedules. They plan school events. They also help with **discipline** and safety.

A principal meets with teachers to make sure they are doing their jobs well.

A superintendent is in charge of a whole **school district**. He or she makes plans for all of the schools in that area. Part of this job involves hiring teachers. It also involves choosing what programs schools will have. In addition, the superintendent decides how schools use their money.

Other administration jobs are at colleges. These jobs can focus on several different areas. In higher education, schools are led by presidents. Deans and provosts help presidents make decisions. For example, they help hire professors and other staff. They also oversee the research that professors do.

Superintendents try to get more money for schools so that students can have better equipment.

Admissions jobs focus on getting new students to attend the college. These jobs often involve travel. Workers may visit high schools. Or they may host events for students. People in admissions also give tours to visitors.

The registrar's office keeps records about students and classes. Its employees plan where and when classes will happen. They help students sign up for classes and get ready to graduate. They also help with **transcripts**.

Other jobs provide resources for students. For example, some people are

RESIDENT DIRECTORS

Resident directors (RDs) watch over students in college dorms. RDs often live in these buildings. They help students with **maintenance** and other problems. RDs often supervise and train resident assistants (RAs). These students are in charge of part of a building, such as a hall or floor. Many RDs worked as RAs when they were in college.

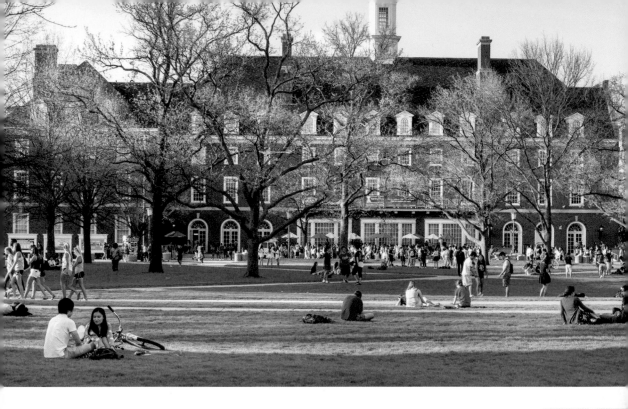

A large college may have thousands of employees.

in charge of student housing. They assign rooms and roommates. They also help take care of the school's buildings. Other workers are in charge of planning events and activities. They help with student groups and clubs. They try to make all students feel included and welcome.

CHAPTER 4

CREATING CURRICULA

Some jobs focus on how students learn. For example, most states and countries have education standards. Standards tell what information students should learn and when they should learn it. To create standards, people study how students learn. They also research what people need to know. They use

Each grade level has a different set of education standards for specific subjects.

this information to create guidelines for schools.

Curricula are how schools apply these guidelines. People make many different kinds of curricula for teachers to use. They write books, websites, lesson plans, and more. Some curricula focus on specific topics, such as reading or

FUN AND FIELD TRIPS

People use curricula outside the classroom. For example, some classes go on field trips. They visit museums, nature centers, zoos, and more. Workers at these places create activities for students. They design plans for students of different ages. Other workers run after-school programs. They plan activities that are both educational and fun.

Field trips help students gain knowledge and experiences that they could not get in the classroom.

science. Others are for certain grades or types of students.

Some jobs look at the school system as a whole. People study what is working well. They also look for problems. They suggest changes or improvements. Other people create standardized tests. These tests help compare students in different places.

SCHOOL LIBRARIAN

School librarians work in elementary, middle, and high schools. They work with both students and teachers. They show students how to use the library's resources and technology. And they help teachers use the library's resources in their classrooms.

Librarians can also work at colleges. They help students and staff find information. At large colleges, librarians may focus on a specific subject, such as law or science. They help people do research on this topic.

Librarians manage the library's resources. They keep everything organized. And they choose new things to buy. These items may include books, videos, and more. Librarians also plan the library's events. They may host clubs or classes.

Librarians make sure students have access to the information they need.

To become school librarians, people must attend college. They usually get a master's degree in library science. This degree helps people learn about research and organization.

CHAPTER 5

ENTERING THE FIELD

For careers in education, the type of training depends on the position. It also varies based on the state or school district. Most jobs require a bachelor's degree in education.

In education classes, people learn about different subjects. They also learn how to explain those subjects to students.

Many careers in education require a four-year college degree.

Some classes focus on a specific age of student. Classes also teach education standards. People practice making lesson plans to meet those standards.

An education degree also involves student teaching. For this step, people go to actual classrooms. They start by observing the teacher and helping with certain tasks. Over time, they begin teaching on their own.

Some jobs have extra requirements. Counselors need to study psychology. Jobs at colleges often require a master's or doctorate degree. And to be deans or principals, people usually need several years of work experience.

People who work in education need to be patient and adaptable. Also, they often work on teams. So, it's important for them to communicate well and share knowledge with others. All these traits help workers best serve students.

CAREER PREP CHECKLIST

Interested in a career in education? As you move into middle school and high school, try these steps.

1 Notice your favorite subjects in school. Look for opportunities to tutor others in these subjects.

2 Work or volunteer with different ages of children to find what ages you enjoy most.

3 Tell your school's guidance counselor about your interest. This person can help you learn more about teaching and education.

4 See if your area has summer camps or after-school programs where you can volunteer. Use the internet to find these opportunities.

5 Learn how to speak and write at least one other language.

FOCUS ON
GREAT CAREERS
IN EDUCATION

Write your answers on a separate piece of paper.

1. Write a paragraph explaining the main ideas of Chapter 4.

2. Which career in education do you think you would enjoy the most? Why?

3. Which person helps students decide on colleges and get ready to graduate?

   A. speech-language pathologist
   B. school counselor
   C. superintendent

4. Why would working in admissions involve traveling?

   A. Workers try to meet many students and tell them about the college.
   B. Workers try to prevent students from visiting the college.
   C. Workers try to spend as much money as possible.

Answer key on page 32.

GLOSSARY

budgets
Plans for how money will be used.

curricula
Plans for teaching certain topics, as well as the books or other materials used to do so.

discipline
The process of training people to follow rules, as well as the consequences when rules are broken.

hygiene
Tasks that help keep the body clean and healthy.

maintenance
The process of fixing, cleaning, and taking care of a building.

refer
To send someone on to an expert who can help.

school district
An area of land where all the schools are grouped together. A district can be part of a city, or it can include several towns.

transcripts
Records of what classes students have taken and the grades they received.

TO LEARN MORE

BOOKS

Ford, Jeanne Marie. *Life with Autism*. Mankato, MN: The Child's World, 2018.

Kistler, Marguerite A. *Working in Education*. Mankato, MN: 12-Story Library, 2018.

Rechner, Amy. *The Department of Education: A Look Behind the Scenes.* North Mankato, MN: Capstone Press, 2019.

NOTE TO EDUCATORS

Visit **www.focusreaders.com** to find lesson plans, activities, links, and other resources related to this title.

INDEX

Answer Key: 1. Answers will vary; **2.** Answers will vary; **3.** B; **4.** A